# PRIMARY MATHEMATICS

**Standards Edition**

1A

## TESTS

**Viya Ayadurai**

mc **Marshall Cavendish** Education

# Preface

Primary Mathematics (Standards Edition) Tests is a series of assessment books.

This series is aligned with the standards adopted by the California State Board of Education and follows the topical arrangement in the Primary Mathematics (Standards Edition) Textbooks. Each chapter comprises Test A and Test B, and each unit concludes with similarly structured Cumulative Tests.

Test A consists of free response questions and assesses students' grasp of mathematical concepts while developing problem-solving skills. Test B is optional and consists of multiple-choice questions aimed at testing students' comprehension of key concepts. As such, it may be used as a retest if teachers perceive the need.

In Cumulative Tests A and B, questions from earlier units are incorporated into each test. These tests focus on review and consolidation through the integration of concepts and strands.

Primary Mathematics (Standards Edition) Tests aims to provide teachers with a set of structured assessment tools for the systematic evaluation of students' learning so as to better understand their individual needs.

# Contents

**Test A**

**Unit 1:** Numbers 0 to 10

**Chapter 1:** Counting

1.  Write the numbers.

2.  Color the correct number of stars.

3. Color the box that shows the correct number.

2

5

4. Write the missing number.

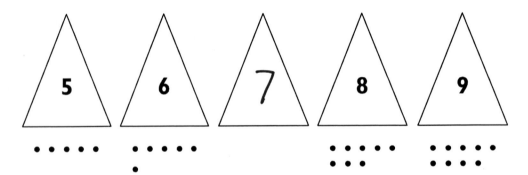

5. Fill in the blanks.

(a) Pablo has ___10___ robots.

(b) He has ___7___ cars.

(c) Does he have more robots or cars? ___robots___

Primary Mathematics (Standards Edition) Tests 1A

6. Count backwards.
   Help Jon find his cat by filling in the missing numbers.

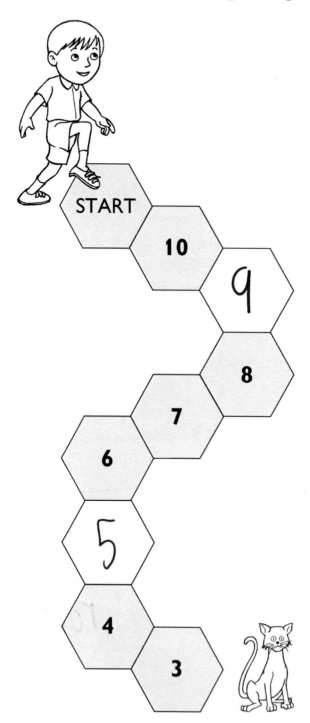

START

10

9

8

7

6

5

4

3

**Test B**

**Unit 1:** Numbers 0 to 10

**Chapter 1:** Counting

Circle the correct option, **A**, **B**, **C** or **D**.

1. Which number is spelled 'three'?

    **A**  3              **C**  7          ?

    **B**  5              **D**  9

2. How many kites are there?

    **A**  4              **C**  6

    **B**  5              **D**  7

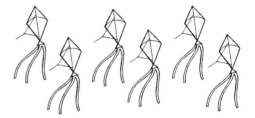

3. There are __5__ crayons.

    **A**  3              **C**  5

    **B**  4              **D**  6

4. What is the missing number?

    ( 0 )  ( 1 )  ( 2 )  ( ? )  ( 4 )  ( 5 )

    **A**  3              **C**  8

    **B**  6              **D**  9

5. The missing number on the clock is _____.

   **A**   4           **(C)**   7

   **B**   5           **D**   9

6. 5 apples are more than __4__ apples.

   **(A)**   4           **C**   6

   **B**   5           **D**   7

7. __0__ is less than 1.

   **(A)**   0           **C**   3

   **B**   2           **D**   4

8. Count on.
   Which number comes next?

   **A**   5           **C**   9

   **(B)**   8           **D**   10

| 6 | 7 | ? |
|---|---|---|

9. Count on.
   What is the missing number?

   **A**   1           **(C)**   4

   **B**   2           **D**   6

| 3 | ? | 5 |
|---|---|---|

10. Count backwards.
    What is the missing number?

   **A**   5           **C**   7

   **B**   6           **(D)**   8

| 10 | 9 | ? |
|----|---|---|

Primary Mathematics (Standards Edition) Tests 1A

**10**

**Chapter 1:** Making Number Stories

1. There are 10 boys.

   7 of them do not wear glasses.

   How many boys wear glasses?

   _____ boys wear glasses.

2. Draw the missing part.

  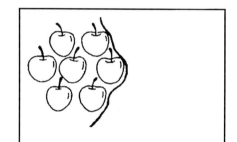

3. Write the missing number.

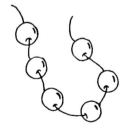 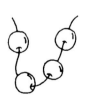 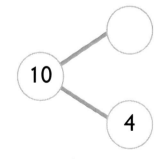

10

4

4. Color the glasses that make 4.

5. Match each teapot with its lid to make 8.

6. Write the missing number.

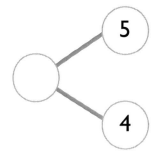

7. 3 and 4 make _____.

Primary Mathematics (Standards Edition) Tests 1A

**Test B**

## Unit 2: Number Bonds

## Chapter 1: Making Number Stories

Circle the correct option, **A**, **B**, **C** or **D**.

1. ●●●● and ●● make _____.

    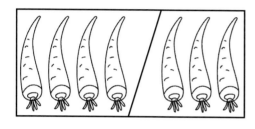

   | | |
   |---|---|
   | **A** 3 | **C** 6 |
   | **B** 5 | **D** 7 |

2. What is the missing number?

    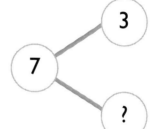

   | | |
   |---|---|
   | **A** 3 | **C** 5 |
   | **B** 4 | **D** 6 |

3. How many marbles does Tom have
   to place in the box to make 10?

   | | |
   |---|---|
   | **A** 5 | **C** 7 |
   | **B** 6 | **D** 8 |

    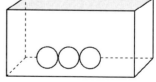

4. What is the missing number?

   | | |
   |---|---|
   | **A** 2 | **C** 4 |
   | **B** 3 | **D** 5 |

    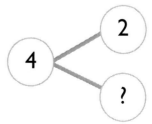

5. Mrs. Davis has 5 oranges.
   3 oranges are rotten.

   _____ oranges are not rotten.

   **A** 2            **C** 4

   **B** 3            **D** 5

6. 5 and _____ make 8.

   **A** 0            **C** 3

   **B** 2            **D** 4

7. To make 9, we need 8 and _____.

   **A** 0            **C** 2

   **B** 1            **D** 3

8. Which pair of numbers makes 10?

   **A** 6 and 4         **C** 2 and 3

   **B** 3 and 5         **D** 4 and 5

9. 5 and 4 make _____.

   **A** 6            **C** 8

   **B** 7            **D** 9

10. 2 and _____ make 2.

   **A** 0            **C** 2

   **B** 1            **D** 3

Primary Mathematics (Standards Edition) Tests 1A

© 2008 Marshall Cavendish International (Singapore) Private Limited

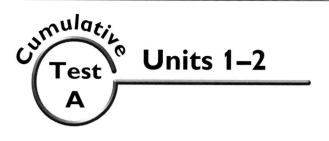

**Cumulative Test A** **Units 1–2**

1. How many balls are there?

Check  the correct answer.

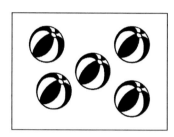

Four   Five   Eight

☐ ☐ ☐

2. How many clowns are there?
   Write the number in words.

_____

3. Color the correct number of cups.

6

*Primary Mathematics (Standards Edition) Tests 1A*

4. Check ✔ the correct set.

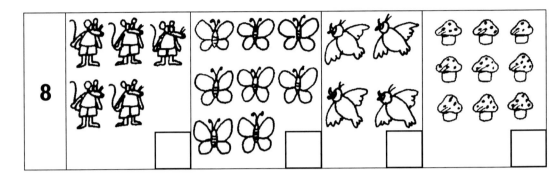

5. Check ✔ the set that has less.

6. Draw a line to show the two parts.

(a)          (b)

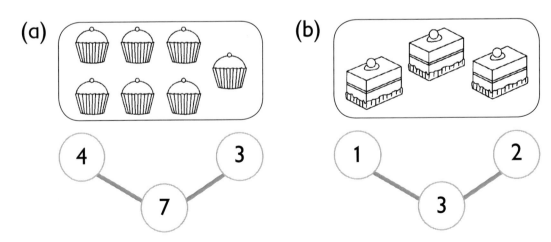

Primary Mathematics (Standards Edition) Tests 1A

© 2008 Marshall Cavendish International (Singapore) Private Limited

7. Draw the missing part.

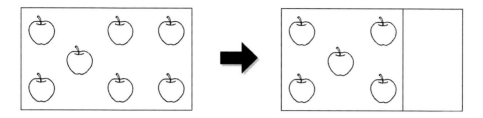

8. Write the missing number.

9. Count backwards.
   Write the missing numbers.

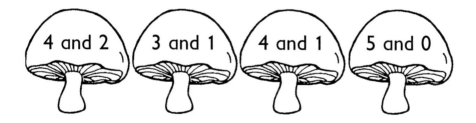

10. Color the mushroom that makes 4.

4 and 2   3 and 1   4 and 1   5 and 0

11. Color two cups that make 7.

Primary Mathematics (Standards Edition) Tests 1A

12. Color the apples that make 9.

13. Write the missing number.

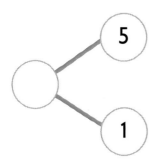

14. Write the missing numbers.

(a)

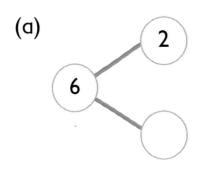

(b)

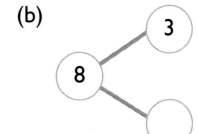

(c)

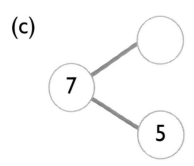

(d)

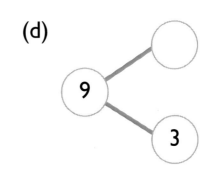

Primary Mathematics (Standards Edition) Tests 1A

## Test B — Units 1–2

Circle the correct option, **A**, **B**, **C** or **D**.

1.  How many vases are there?

    **A**  5          **C**  7
    **B**  6          **D**  8

2.  Which set has 5 objects?

    **A**

    **B**

    **C**

    **D**

3.  Count backwards.
    What is the missing number?

    | 8 | ? | 6 | 5 |

    **A**  3          **C**  7
    **B**  4          **D**  9

4.  What is the missing number?

    **A**  1          **C**  3
    **B**  2          **D**  4

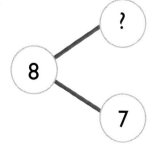

Primary Mathematics (Standards Edition) Tests 1A

5. What is the missing number?

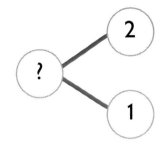

   **A**   1          **C**   3

   **B**   2          **D**   4

6. Which number is less than  ?

   **A**   4          **C**   6

   **B**   5          **D**   7

7. Which number is more than  ?

   **A**   4          **C**   6

   **B**   5          **D**   8

8. 3 and 6 make _____ .

   **A**   7          **C**   9

   **B**   8          **D**   10

9. Which numbers make 7?

   **A**   2 and 1          **C**   5 and 4

   **B**   3 and 2          **D**   4 and 3

10. 6 and _____ make 8.

   **A**   1          **C**   3

   **B**   2          **D**   4

Primary Mathematics (Standards Edition) Tests 1A

## Test A

## Unit 3: Addition

## Chapter 1: Making Addition Stories

1.

Emma has 5 books.
Janet gives Emma 4 books.

Emma has _____ books altogether.

2. Fill in the missing numbers.

(a)

4 + 3 = _____

(b)

6 + 3 = _____

Primary Mathematics (Standards Edition) Tests 1A

3. Write two addition sentences for the picture.

_____ + _____ = 8

_____ + _____ = 8

Primary Mathematics (Standards Edition) Tests 1A

© 2008 Marshall Cavendish International (Singapore) Private Limited

### Test B

## Unit 3: Addition

## Chapter 1: Making Addition Stories

Circle the correct option, **A**, **B**, **C** or **D**.

1.  5 + 3 = _____

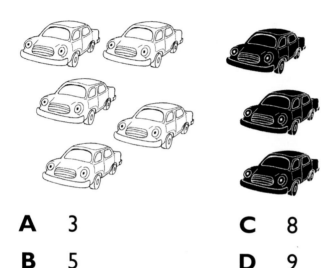

| **A** | 3 | **C** | 8 |
|---|---|---|---|
| **B** | 5 | **D** | 9 |

2.  Whitney has 4 guppies.
    She has 2 goldfish.

How many fish does she have altogether?
4 + 2 = _____

| **A** | 8 | **C** | 4 |
|---|---|---|---|
| **B** | 6 | **D** | 2 |

3. What are the missing numbers?

_____ + _____ = 7

**A**   3 and 4        **C**   4 and 1

**B**   2 and 3        **D**   3 and 3

4. Which is the correct addition sentence?

**A**   5 + 0 = 5        **C**   3 + 2 = 5

**B**   4 + 1 = 5        **D**   1 + 4 = 5

5. How many apples are there?

5 + _____ = 9

**A**   3                **C**   7

**B**   4                **D**   9

Test A — **Unit 3:** Addition

**Chapter 2:** Addition with Number Bonds

1.  Write the missing number.

6 + 2 = ?

2.  Draw the missing ♡ and write the missing number.

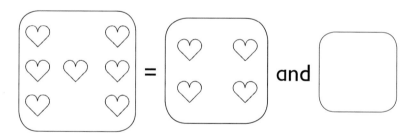

7 = 4 + _____

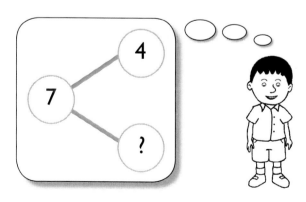

Primary Mathematics (Standards Edition) Tests 1A

3. Write the missing number.

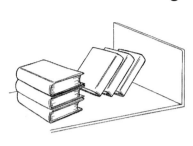

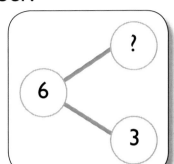

_____ + 3 = 6

4. Draw more flags to make 5.
Write the missing numbers in the number bond.

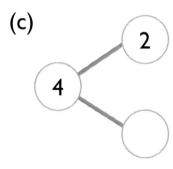

5. Write the missing number.

(a)

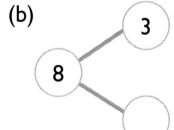

2 1

(b)

8 3

(c)

4 2

6. Complete the addition sentences.

7 + 2 = _____          2 + 7 = _____

Primary Mathematics (Standards Edition) Tests 1A          © 2008 Marshall Cavendish International (Singapore) Private Limited

5

**Test B**

# Unit 3: Addition

## Chapter 2: Addition with Number Bonds

Circle the correct option, **A**, **B**, **C** or **D**.

1. What is the missing number?

+ _____ =

  **A**   1             **C**   3

  **B**   2             **D**   4

2. $3 + 4 =$ _____

The missing number is _____.

  **A**   3             **C**   7

  **B**   4             **D**   9

3. Which numbers make 8?

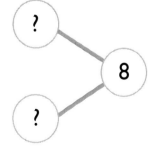

  **A**   5 and 3       **C**   4 and 2

  **B**   6 and 3       **D**   5 and 2

4. What is the missing number?

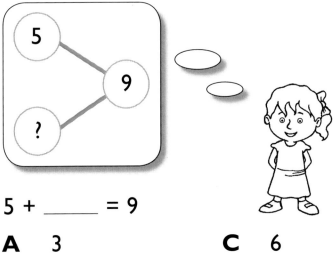

5 + _____ = 9

**A**  3                    **C**  6

**B**  4                    **D**  7

5. What is the missing number?

_____ + 3 = 10

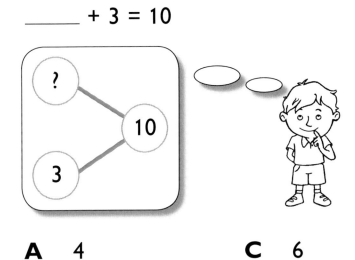

**A**  4                    **C**  6

**B**  5                    **D**  7

Primary Mathematics (Standards Edition) Tests 1A

© 2008 Marshall Cavendish International (Singapore) Private Limited

## Test A

### Unit 3: Addition

### Chapter 3: Other Methods of Addition

1. Write the missing number.

7 + _____ = 10

2. Write the missing number.

6 + 3 = _____

3. Write the missing numbers.

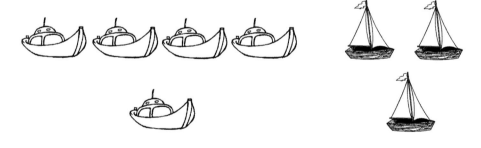

_____ + _____ = _____

4. Count on to add 5 and 2.
   Color the correct box.

| 3 | 4 | 5 | 6 | 7 | 8 | 9 | 10 |
|---|---|---|---|---|---|---|----|

Primary Mathematics (Standards Edition) Tests 1A

5. Complete the addition sentences.

(a) $6 + 1 =$ _____

(b) $7 + 2 =$ _____

(c) $4 + 3 =$ _____

(d) $5 + 4 =$ _____

6. Add 9 and 0.

The answer is _____.

7. Write the missing numbers.

(a) _____ $+ 1 = 10$

(b) $8 +$ _____ $= 10$

(c) _____ $+ 5 = 10$

(d) $6 +$ _____ $= 10$

8. Tim had 4 grapefruits.
He bought 4 more grapefruits.

$4 + 4 =$ _____

He had _____ grapefruits altogether.

Primary Mathematics (Standards Edition) Tests 1A

## Test B

## Unit 3: Addition

## Chapter 3: Other Methods of Addition

Circle the correct option, **A**, **B**, **C** or **D**.

1.  Count on to add 3 and 2. What is the answer?

| 1 | 2 | 3 | 4 | 5 | 6 | 7 | 8 |

   **A**  2           **C**  4

   **B**  3           **D**  5

2.  $7 + 3 =$ _____

   **A**  3           **C**  7

   **B**  5           **D**  10

3.  $6 +$ _____ $= 10$

   **A**  4           **C**  8

   **B**  6           **D**  10

4.  1 more than _____ is 10.

   **A**  5           **C**  9

   **B**  7           **D**  10

5. There are 8 flowers in a vase.
   Add 2 more.
   How many flowers are there altogether?

   **A**   10          **C**   6

   **B**   8           **D**   4

6. 5 and 5 make _____.

   **A**   4           **C**   7

   **B**   6           **D**   10

7. 6 and _____ make 10.

   **A**   4           **C**   7

   **B**   5           **D**   8

8. 5 + 3 = _____

   **A**   1           **C**   6

   **B**   4           **D**   8

9. 3 more than 4 is _____.

   **A**   5           **C**   7

   **B**   6           **D**   8

10. Add 4 pencils to 5 pencils.
    How many pencils are there?

    **A**   6          **C**   8

    **B**   7          **D**   9

Primary Mathematics (Standards Edition) Tests 1A

© 2008 Marshall Cavendish International (Singapore) Private Limited

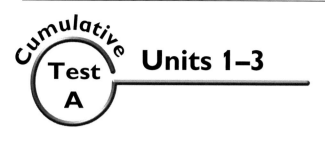

## Cumulative Test A — Units 1–3

1. Count backwards.
   Write the missing numbers.

2. How many boxes are there?

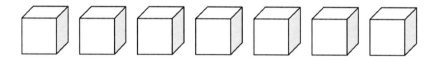

   There are _____ boxes.

3.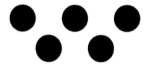

   There are _____ black balls.

   There are _____ white balls.

   There are _____ balls altogether.

4. Draw the total number of  and write the missing number.

 =  and

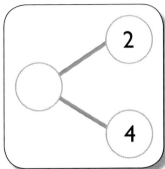

_____ = 2 + 4

5. Complete the addition sentence.

_____ + _____ = _____

6.

There are 4 big butterflies.

There are _____ small butterflies.

There are _____ butterflies altogether.

Primary Mathematics (Standards Edition) Tests 1A

7. What is 2 more than 8?

| 5 | 6 | 7 | 8 | 9 | 10 |
|---|---|---|---|---|----|

   The answer is _____.

8. 1 more than 7 is _____.

9. 2 more than 4 is _____.

10. 3 more than 6 is _____.

11. 3 more than 7 is _____.

12. Write the missing numbers.

   (a) 6 + _____ = 9

   (b) 3 + _____ = 9

   (c) 4 + _____ = 9

13. Use the numbers below to fill in the blanks.

| 3 | 2 | 1 | 0 |
|---|---|---|---|

   _____ and _____ make 3.

   _____ and _____ also make 3.

Blank

## Cumulative Test B — Units 1–3

Circle the correct option, **A**, **B**, **C** or **D**.

1. How many apples are there altogether?

**A** 10          **C** 8

**B** 9           **D** 6

2. Count on.

The missing number is _____.

**A** 2           **C** 6

**B** 3           **D** 8

3. How many birds are there?

3 + 5 = _____

**A** 2             **C** 5

**B** 3             **D** 8

4. What is 1 more than 9?

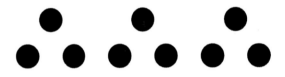

**A** 1             **C** 9

**B** 8             **D** 10

5. What is the missing number?

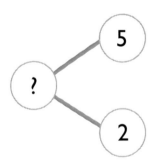

**A** 5             **C** 7

**B** 6             **D** 8

Primary Mathematics (Standards Edition) Tests 1A

6. 5 and 1 is _____.

   **A** 6         **C** 8

   **B** 7         **D** 9

7. 6 + 2 = _____

| 4 | 5 | 6 | 7 | 8 |
|---|---|---|---|---|

   **A** 4         **C** 7

   **B** 6         **D** 8

8. 3 + 2 = _____

   **A** 1         **C** 4

   **B** 3         **D** 5

9. Jim has 2 basketballs.
   He buys 2 more.
   How many basketballs does he have now?

   **A** 3         **C** 5

   **B** 4         **D** 6

Turn the page.

Primary Mathematics (Standards Edition) Tests 1A

10. Which is the correct addition sentence?

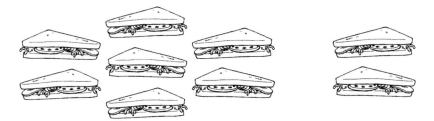

_____ ◯ _____ = _____

**A**   7 + 3 = 10         **C**   3 + 5 = 8

**B**   7 + 2 = 9          **D**   3 + 4 = 7

**Test A**

# Unit 4: Subtraction

## Chapter 1: Making Subtraction Stories

1. Fill in the blank.

There are **9** butterflies.
**4** fly away.

_____ butterflies are left.

2. Fill in the blank.

_____ apples are left.

3. Write the missing number.

4 – 1 = _____

Complete the number sentences and fill in the blanks for questions 4 to 6.

4.   There are 7 buckets.
     Mary takes away 2 buckets.

     7 – _____ = _____

     _____ buckets are left.

5.   There are 6 children playing together.

     4 of them are boys.

     _____ – 4 = _____

     There are _____ girls.

6.   There are 5 cats.

     3 are eating.

     How many cats are sleeping?

     _____ ◯ _____ = _____

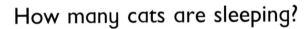

     _____ cats are sleeping.

Primary Mathematics (Standards Edition) Tests 1A

© 2008 Marshall Cavendish International (Singapore) Private Limited

**Test B**

# Unit 4: Subtraction

## Chapter 1: Making Subtraction Stories

Circle the correct option, **A**, **B**, **C** or **D**.

1. There are 7 children.
   2 of them have bags.
   How many children do not have bags?

   7 − 2 = \_\_\_\_\_

   **A**  3              **C**  5

   **B**  4              **D**  9

2. How many eggs did Janet cook?

   9 − 6 = \_\_\_\_\_

   **A**  2              **C**  5

   **B**  3              **D**  7

Primary Mathematics (Standards Edition) Tests 1A

3. 6 − 2 = _____

    **A**  0        **C**  4

    **B**  1        **D**  8

4. 10 − 2 = _____

    **A**  5        **C**  8

    **B**  6        **D**  10

5. There are 5 frogs.
   4 hop away.
   Which is the correct number sentence?

    **A**  4 + 0 = 4      **C**  5 − 4 = 1

    **B**  5 − 1 = 4      **D**  5 + 4 = 9

Primary Mathematics (Standards Edition) Tests 1A

**Test A** | **Unit 4:** Subtraction

**Chapter 2:** Methods of Subtraction

1. Tara has 6 apples.

   She eats 3 apples.

   How many apples are left?

   6 – 3 = __3__

2. Complete the number sentence and fill in the blank.

   Mr. Clark has 5 eggs.

   He eats 2 of them.

   5 $\bigcirc$ 2 = __3__

   He has __3__ eggs left.

3. Subtract 1 from 6 and fill in the blank.

   6 – 1 = __5__

   | 3 | 4 | 5 | 6 | 7 | 8 | 9 | 10 |

4. Write the missing number.

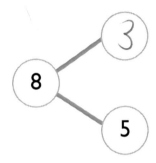

5. Complete the subtraction sentences.

(a) 4 – 4 = ___0___

(b) 4 – 2 = ___2___

(c) 4 – 0 = ___4___

(d) 7 – 3 = ___4___

(e) 9 – 3 = ___6___

Primary Mathematics (Standards Edition) Tests 1A                    © 2008 Marshall Cavendish International (Singapore) Private Limited

5

**Test B**

**Unit 4:** Subtraction

**Chapter 2:** Methods of Subtraction

Circle the correct option, **A**, **B**, **C** or **D**.

1. Jon and Miguel have 10 pencils altogether.
   Miguel has 5 pencils.
   How many pencils does Jon have?

| | | | |
|---|---|---|---|
| **A** | 3 | **C** | 8 |
| **(B)** | 5 | **D** | 10 |

2. What is the missing number?

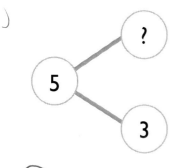 

| | | | |
|---|---|---|---|
| **(A)** | 2 | **C** | 5 |
| **B** | 3 | **D** | 7 |

3. Subtract 2 from 9.

   9 − 2 = _____

   **A**  2              **C**  8

   **B**  7              **D**  10

4. What is the missing number?

   6 − _____ = 3

   **A**  3              **C**  6

   **B**  5              **D**  9

5. Rhonda bought 10 eggs.
   She fell and 3 eggs broke.
   How many eggs did she have left?
   Which is the correct number sentence?

   **A**  7 + 3 = 10        **C**  10 − 7 = 3

   **B**  3 + 7 = 10        **D**  10 − 3 = 7

Primary Mathematics (Standards Edition) Tests 1A                    © 2008 Marshall Cavendish International (Singapore) Private Limited

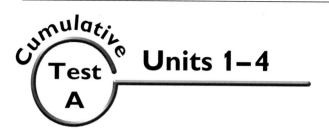

**Cumulative Test A**   **Units 1–4**

1. Count on.

   Write the missing numbers.

3    4    ☁    6    ☁

2. There are 8 toy airplanes.

   5 are broken.

   _____ airplanes are left.

3.

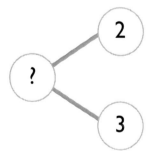

2

?

3

   2 penguins are swimming.

   3 penguins join them.

   There are _____ penguins altogether.

Primary Mathematics (Standards Edition) Tests 1A

4. Draw the missing △ and write the missing number.

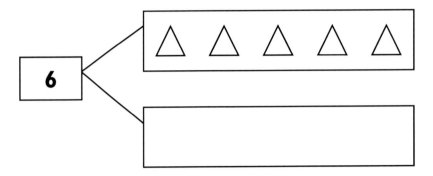

6 – 5 = _____

5. Subtract 4 from 10.

| 3 | 4 | 5 | 6 | 7 | 8 | 9 | 10 |
|---|---|---|---|---|---|---|----|

The answer is _____.

6. Write the missing number.

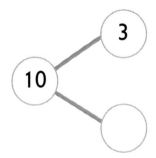

Primary Mathematics (Standards Edition) Tests 1A

7. Complete the number sentences.

(a) 7 + 3 = _____

(b) 2 + 4 = _____

(c) 9 – 6 = _____

(d) 10 – 7 = _____

8. Color the hearts that make 9.

9. Complete the addition sentences using the numbers.

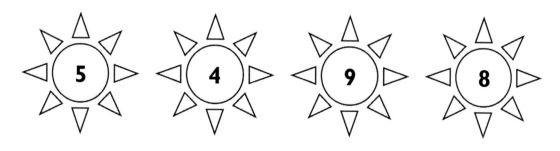

_____ + 5 = 9

1 + _____ = 10

Primary Mathematics (Standards Edition) Tests 1A

10. Complete the subtraction sentences using the numbers. Do not use the numbers more than once.

| 3 | 9 | 1 | 10 | 2 |

_____ − _____ = 1

_____ − _____ = 1

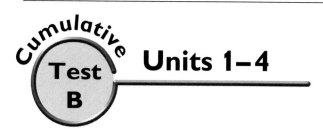

## Cumulative Test B — Units 1–4

Circle the correct option, **A**, **B**, **C** or **D**.

1. How many flowers are there?

   **A** 6          **C** 9

   **B** 8          **D** 10

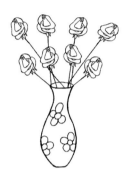

2. There were 4 birds on a tree.
   2 flew away.
   How many birds are left?

   **A** 1          **C** 3

   **B** 2          **D** 4

3. There are 5 stars altogether.
   How many stars are white?

   **A** 2          **C** 4

   **B** 3          **D** 5

4. Complete the number sentence.

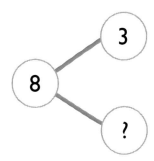

6 + 3 = _____

A   3              C   6

B   5              D   9

5. What is the missing number?

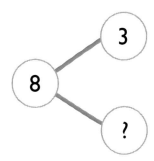

A   5              C   7

B   6              D   8

6. Complete the addition sentence.

6 + 1 = _____

A   4              C   7

B   6              D   8

Primary Mathematics (Standards Edition) Tests 1A

© 2008 Marshall Cavendish International (Singapore) Private Limited

7. 7 and 0 make _____.

   **A** 7           **C** 9

   **B** 8           **D** 10

8. There are 9 rabbits.

   How many rabbits do not have carrots?
   Which is the correct subtraction sentence?

   **A** 9 – 5 = 4        **C** 9 – 3 = 6

   **B** 9 – 4 = 5        **D** 9 – 2 = 7

9. Take away 3 from 9.
   The answer is _____.

   **A** 4           **C** 6

   **B** 5           **D** 8

10. What is the missing number?

    10 – _____ = 4

    **A** 2           **C** 6

    **B** 4           **D** 8

Blank

**Points**

**10**

**Test A**  **Unit 5:** Position

**Chapter 1:** Position and Direction

1. Fill in the blanks.

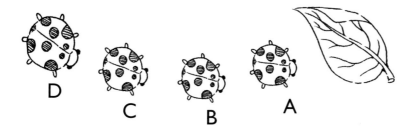

(a) Beetle _____ is **behind** Beetle C.

(b) The leaf is **in front of** Beetle _____.

Circle the correct answers.

(c) Beetle C is (near / far from) Beetle D.

(d) Beetle D is (near / far from) the leaf.

2. Circle the correct answers.

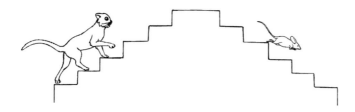

(a) The cat is running (under / up / down) the stairs.

(b) The mouse is running (below / down / up) the stairs.

3.  Help James find his friends.

Fill in the blanks with the words given.

| left | under | behind | right | next to |
|------|-------|--------|-------|---------|

(a) Sean is hiding _____ the bed.

(b) Lee is on the _____ of the picture.

(c) Sally is on the _____ of the picture.

(d) James is standing _____ the bed.

5

**Test B** — **Unit 5:** Position

**Chapter 1:** Position and Direction

Circle the correct option, **A**, **B**, **C** or **D**.

1. Betty is on the _____.

  **A**    far              **C**    right

  **B**    left             **D**    behind

2. The teacher is _____ the students.

  **A**    next to        **C**    behind

  **B**    far from       **D**    in front of

Primary Mathematics (Standards Edition) Tests 1A

3. The cat is sleeping _____ the table.

**A** under    **C** in front of

**B** above    **D** far

4. The basketball net is _____ Sam.

**A** down    **C** under

**B** above    **D** below

5. Rita is sitting _____ the bird.

**A** up    **C** next to

**B** down    **D** below

**Test A**    **Unit 5:** Position

**Chapter 2:** Ordinal Numbers — Naming Position

1. Color the 6th house.

1st

2. Color the fourth tree.

1st

3. Draw a fish in the 2nd bowl from the right.

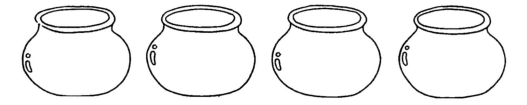

4. Color the fifth bucket from the left.

Primary Mathematics (Standards Edition) Tests 1A

5. Color the 9th flag from the right.

6. Circle the eighth bird from the left.

7. (a) Match the labels to the runners.

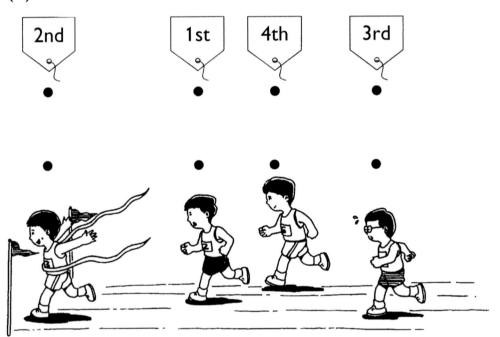

(b) Write the ordinal numbers in words.

_____    _____    _____    _____
        1st                  2nd                  3rd                  4th

Primary Mathematics (Standards Edition) Tests 1A
© 2008 Marshall Cavendish International (Singapore) Private Limited

Name: Class: Date:

Points

5

**Test B**

# Unit 5: Position

**Chapter 2:** Ordinal Numbers — Naming Position

Circle the correct option, **A**, **B**, **C** or **D**.

1.

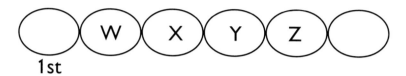

What letter is in the 4th bubble?

**A** W **C** Y

**B** X **D** Z

2.

Star _____ is 5th from the right.

**A** P **C** R

**B** Q **D** S

3.

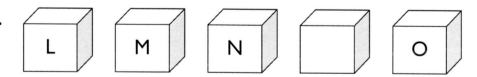

Box _____ is 3rd from the left.

**A** L **C** N

**B** M **D** O

**4.**

| 2 | 3 | 4 | 5 | 6 | 7 |
|---|---|---|---|---|---|

Which number is sixth from the right?

**A**  2          **C**  6

**B**  3          **D**  7

**5.**

Which is the 4th letter?

**A**  E          **C**  P

**B**  O          **D**  R

20

**Test A**    **Units 1–5**

1. The number after 6 is _____ .

2. Write the missing number in the ⬡ .

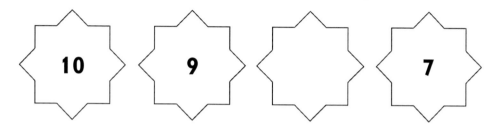

10     9        7

3. Rick has 4 bags.
   2 are small.
   The rest are big.
   How many big bags does Rick have?

   Rick has _____ big bags.

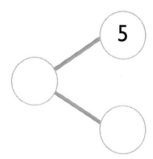

4. Look at the picture.
   Write the missing numbers.

5

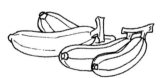

Primary Mathematics (Standards Edition) Tests 1A

5. Write the missing number.

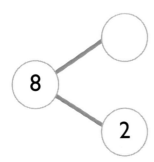

6. Complete the addition and subtraction sentences.

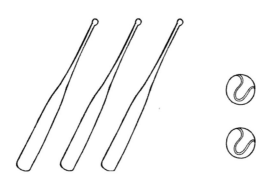

3 + _____ = _____

_____ − 3 = _____

7. Complete the number sentences.

(a) 6 + 3 = _____

(b) 7 + 2 = _____

(c) 9 − 5 = _____

(d) 10 − 6 = _____

Primary Mathematics (Standards Edition) Tests 1A
© 2008 Marshall Cavendish International (Singapore) Private Limited

8.  Use these words to help you fill in the blanks.

| under | right | left | above |
|---|---|---|---|

Thomas

(a) The tree is on the _____ side of the picture.

(b) The dog is _____ the tree.

(c) Thomas is on the _____ side of the picture.

(d) The cloud is _____ Thomas.

9.  Color the 5th shape from the left.

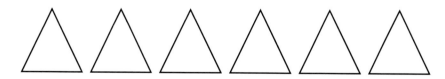

Primary Mathematics (Standards Edition) Tests 1A

10. Color the 2nd ball from the right.

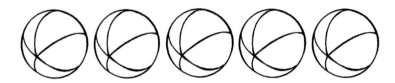

11. Fill in the blanks.

(a) 1st, 2nd, _____, 4th, 5th

(b) seventh, eighth, _____, tenth

(c) fifth, _____, seventh, eighth

## Cumulative Test B — Units 1–5

Circle the correct option, **A**, **B**, **C** or **D**.

1. How many dots are there?

| | | | |
|---|---|---|---|
| **A** 5 | | **C** 8 | |
| **B** 6 | | **D** 9 | |

2. What is the missing number?

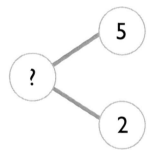

| | | | |
|---|---|---|---|
| **A** 5 | | **C** 7 | |
| **B** 6 | | **D** 8 | |

3. What is the missing number?

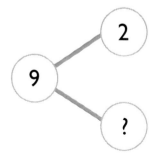

| | | | |
|---|---|---|---|
| **A** 3 | | **C** 6 | |
| **B** 5 | | **D** 7 | |

4. John had 7 oranges.
   He ate 2 of them.

   He has _____ oranges left.

   **A** 5          **C** 8

   **B** 6          **D** 9

5. What is 3 more than 0?

   **A** 0          **C** 2

   **B** 1          **D** 3

6. Take away 2 from 10.
   What is the answer?

   **A** 10         **C** 8

   **B** 9          **D** 7

7. Sally has 3 red buttons.
   She has 7 blue buttons.

   She has _____ buttons altogether.

   **A** 4          **C** 8

   **B** 5          **D** 10

Primary Mathematics (Standards Edition) Tests 1A

© 2008 Marshall Cavendish International (Singapore) Private Limited

Look at the picture to answer questions 8 to 11.

8. Amy is _____ Jeff.

   **A**   behind          **C**   far from

   **B**   next to         **D**   under

9. Jason is _____ Amy and Jeff.

   **A**   in front of     **C**   behind

   **B**   beside          **D**   above

10. The tree is _____ the house.

   **A**   far from        **C**   behind

   **B**   near            **D**   beside

11. The bird is flying _____ the tree.

   **A**   under           **C**   down

   **B**   beside          **D**   above

**12.**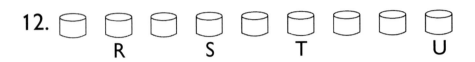

Which container is 4th from the right?

**A** R **C** T

**B** S **D** U

**13.**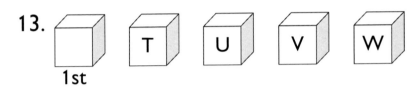

1st

Which is the 4th box?

**A** T **C** V

**B** U **D** W

Look at the picture to answer questions 14 and 15.

Jason   Winona   Tao   Lola

**14.** Tao is _____ from the left.

**A** 1st **C** 3rd

**B** 2nd **D** 4th

**15.** Lola is _____ from the right.

**A** 1st **C** 3rd

**B** 2nd **D** 4th

## Test A

**Unit 6:** Numbers to 20

**Chapter 1:** Counting and Comparing

1. Count and check ✔ the correct number.

 (a)

| 12 | 13 | 14 |
| :-: | :-: | :-: |
| ✓ | ☐ | ☐ |

(b)

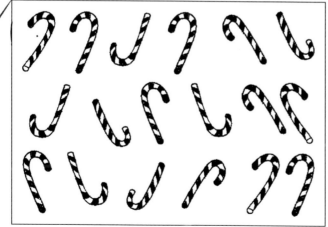

| seventeen | eighteen | nineteen |
| :-: | :-: | :-: |
|  |  ✓ |  |

2. Color 10  and write the missing number.

13 = 10 + ___3___

3. Count backwards.
   Write the missing numbers.

20   19   18   17   16   15

4. Color the leaf with the greatest number.

16   14   18   17   13   15

5. Arrange the numbers in order.
   Write them in the stars.
   Begin with the smallest number.

11        16        9        15

9    11    15    16

smallest

Primary Mathematics (Standards Edition) Tests 1A

© 2008 Marshall Cavendish International (Singapore) Private Limited

6. 10 and 8 is __18__.

7. __10__ + 9 = 19

8. 10 + __10__ = 20

Primary Mathematics (Standards Edition) Tests 1A

Blank

Test B

**Unit 6:** Numbers to 20

**Chapter 1:** Counting and Comparing

Circle the correct option, **A**, **B**, **C** or **D**.

1. How many cherries are there?

   **A**  10       **C**  13

   **B**  12       (**D**)  14

2. Count backwards by 2's.
   What is the missing number?

| 17 | ? | 13 | 11 |

   **A**  12       (**C**)  15

   **B**  14       **D**  16

3. Which of the following is the greatest number?

   **A**  15       **C**  12

   (**B**)  18       **D**  10

4. Which of the following is the smallest number?

   **A**  13       **C**  16

   (**B**)  11       **D**  19

Primary Mathematics (Standards Edition) Tests 1A

5. _____ and 9 is 19.

   (A) 10          C 15

   B 11          D 19

6. 15 is the same as _____.

   A 10 + 1          C 10 + 4

   B 10 + 2          (D) 10 + 5

7. _____ is the same as 10 + 8.

   A 17          C 19

   (B) 18          D 20

8. 10 and _____ is 17.

   A 1          (C) 7

   B 5          D 9

9. 9 + 10 = _____

   A 9          (C) 19

   B 10          D 20

10. Which is the correct addition sentence?

   A 9 + 7 = 16          C 9 + 8 = 17

   (B) 10 + 6 = 16          D 10 + 7 = 17

**Test A** **Unit 6:** Numbers to 20

**Chapter 2:** Addition and Subtraction

1.  Write the missing numbers.

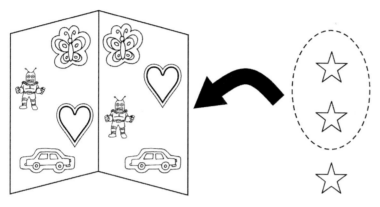

✓ 8 + ③ = __11__

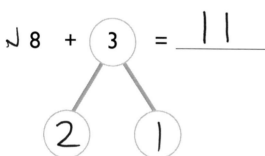

✓
2.  Write the missing number.

    (a)

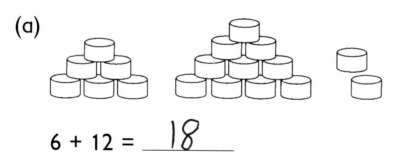

6 + 12 = __18__

(b)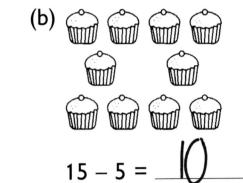

15 − 5 = ___10___

3. Write **+** or **−** in each ◯.

(a) 9 ⊕ 7 = 16

(b) 14 ⊖ 3 = 11

(c) 11 ⊕ 6 = 17

(d) 20 ⊖ 7 = 13

4. 9 + 4 = ___13___

5. ___8___ + 7 = 15

Primary Mathematics (Standards Edition) Tests 1A

© 2008 Marshall Cavendish International (Singapore) Private Limited

6. Write the missing numbers.

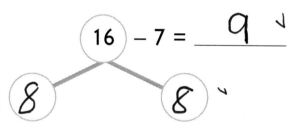

$16 - 7 =$ ___9___ ✓

8      8 ✓

7. $15 - 6 =$ ___9___ ✓

8. Janet has 9 balloons.

She buys 6 more balloons.

How many balloons does Janet have altogether?

✓ $9 + 6 =$ ___15___

✓ Janet has ___15___ balloons altogether.

9. Fred has 18 stamps.

Bob has 9 stamps.

How many more stamps does Fred have?

✓ $18 - 9 =$ ___9___

✓ Fred has ___9___ more stamps.

Blank

**Test B**

**Unit 6:** Numbers to 20

**Chapter 2:** Addition and Subtraction

Circle the correct option, **A**, **B**, **C** or **D**.

1. How many pencils are there?

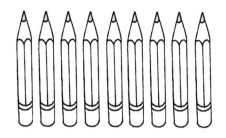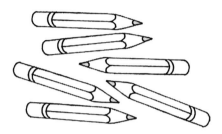

$9 + 6 =$ _____

**A** 13        **C** 15

**B** 14        **D** 16

2. $7 + 5 =$ _____

**A** 8        **C** 11

**B** 10        **D** 12

3. Ron has **8** stickers.
   He buys 5 more.        $8 + 5 = 13$
   How many stickers does he have now?

**A** 8        **C** 13

**B** 12        **D** 15

4. How many tomatoes are there?

14 + 3 = \_\_\_\_\_

A    7           C    15

B    13         (D)   17

5. How many eggs are left?

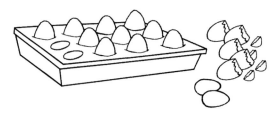

17 − 5 = \_\_\_\_\_

(A)   12         C    17

B    14         D    19

6. Add 12 and 8.
The answer is \_\_\_\_\_.

A    14         C    18

B    16         (D)   20

7. Mrs. Lee has 10 pears.
She buys 6 more.
She has \_\_\_\_\_ pears altogether.

(A)   16         C    19

B    18         D    20

Primary Mathematics (Standards Edition) Tests 1A

8. √ Mr. Green has 15 lemons.
   He sells 3 lemons.
   He has _____ lemons left.

   **A**   11                **C**   13
   (**B**)   12              **D**   14

9. There are 14 apples.
   7 of them are rotten.

   14 − 7 = _____

   _____ apples are not rotten.

   **A**   5                 (**C**   7)
   **B**   6                 **D**   10

10. Subtract 6 from 13.
    What is the answer?

    **A**   6                **C**   10
    (**B**)   7             **D**   19

Primary Mathematics (Standards Edition) Tests 1A

Blank

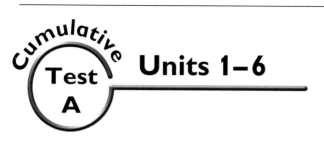

**Cumulative Test A** **Units 1–6**

1. The number that comes before 4 is _____.

2. Color the cloud with numbers that make 7.

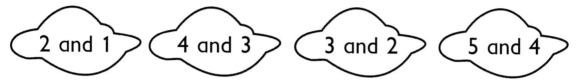

2 and 1    4 and 3    3 and 2    5 and 4

3. Write the missing number.

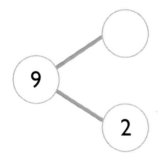

9    2

4. Complete the number sentences.

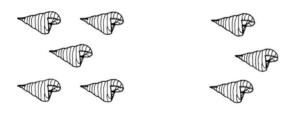

5 + _____ = 8

3 + _____ = 8

5. Color the 3rd ball from the left.

6. Count on or backwards.
   Write the missing numbers.

   (a)
   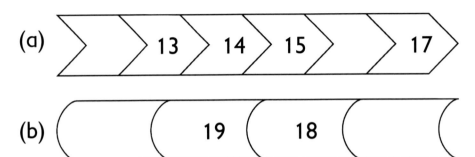

   13  14  15      17

   (b)

   19  18

7. 14 is the same as 10 + _____.

8. What is 3 more than 15?

   The answer is _____.

9. Complete the number sentences.

   (a) 8 + 6 = _____

   (b) 15 + 4 = _____

   (c) 17 − 5 = _____

   (d) 14 − 7 = _____

Primary Mathematics (Standards Edition) Tests 1A

© 2008 Marshall Cavendish International (Singapore) Private Limited

10. There are 15 flowers in a vase.
    Add 5 more.
    How many flowers are there altogether?

    There are _____ flowers altogether.

11. Sid has 12 tubes of paint.
    7 of them are empty.
    How many tubes of paint does he have left?

    He has _____ tubes of paint left.

Blank

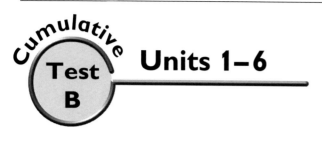

# Cumulative Test B — Units 1–6

Circle the correct option, **A**, **B**, **C** or **D**.

1.  Which number is spelled 'seven'?

   **A**  5              **C**  7

   **B**  6              **D**  9

2.  Which numbers make 10?

   **A**  5 and 3       **C**  6 and 4

   **B**  5 and 4       **D**  6 and 5

3.  Who is 2nd from the right?

   **A**  Sue           **C**  Mei

   **B**  Joe           **D**  Ali

Sue    Joe    Ali    Mei

4.  3 more than 12 is _____.

   **A**  15             **C**  17

   **B**  16             **D**  19

5.  $19 - 3 =$ _____

   **A**  15             **C**  17

   **B**  16             **D**  18

Primary Mathematics (Standards Edition) Tests 1A

6.  5 + 9 = _____

    **A**  11                    **C**  14

    **B**  13                    **D**  15

7.  9 and _____ make 20.

    **A**  11                    **C**  15

    **B**  14                    **D**  17

8.  17 – 8 = _____

    **A**  5                     **C**  7

    **B**  6                     **D**  9

9.  Betty has 15 crayons.
    She gives away 7 crayons.
    How many crayons does she have left?

    **A**  5                     **C**  8

    **B**  6                     **D**  9

10. There are 8 paper planes.
    Tim makes 4 more.

    There are _____ paper planes altogether.

    **A**  12                    **C**  14

    **B**  13                    **D**  15

**Test A** **Unit 7:** Shapes

**Chapter 1:** Common Shapes

1.  Color the shapes that match the objects on the left.

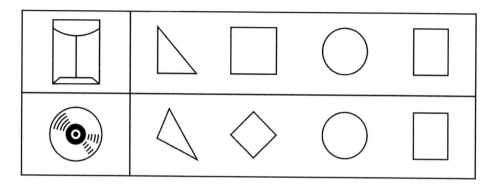

2.  Color the bigger circle.

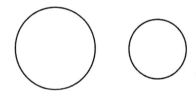

3.  Check ✔ the solid that does **not** have any flat surfaces.

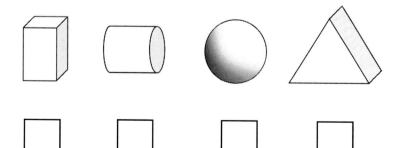

Primary Mathematics (Standards Edition) Tests 1A

4. Color the face that objects can be stacked on.

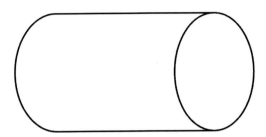

5. Check ✔ the objects that we can slide.

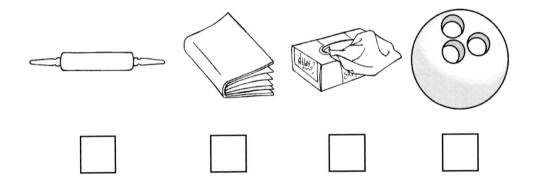

© 2008 Marshall Cavendish International (Singapore) Private Limited

6. Match.

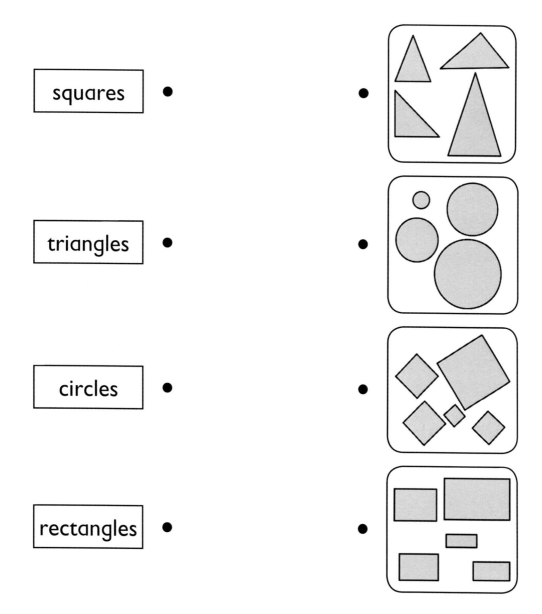

squares •

triangles •

circles •

rectangles •

7. Color the shape that has more sides and corners.

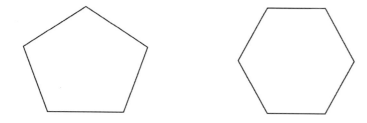

8. The objects are placed in a regular pattern.
   Color the object that comes next.

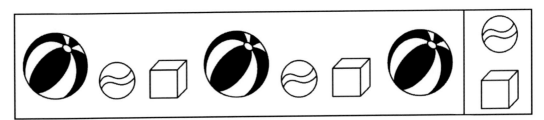

9. Color the two shapes that form a square.

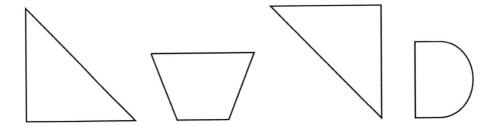

## Test B

## Unit 7: Shapes

## Chapter 1: Common Shapes

Circle the correct option, **A**, **B**, **C** or **D**.

1. How many circles are there?

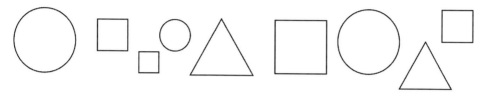

    **A**   1          **C**   3

    **B**   2          **D**   4

2. Which object has **only** flat faces?

    **A**         **C**

    **B**         **D**

3. Which object can we roll?

    **A**         **C**

    **B**         **D**

Primary Mathematics (Standards Edition) Tests 1A

4.  How many corners does this shape have?

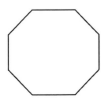

**A**  5          **C**  7

**B**  6          **D**  8

5.  How many sides does this shape have?

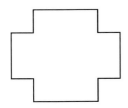

**A**  4          **C**  12

**B**  8          **D**  16

6.  Group by shape.
    How many groups are there?

**A**  2          **C**  5

**B**  3          **D**  8

Primary Mathematics (Standards Edition) Tests 1A

© 2008 Marshall Cavendish International (Singapore) Private Limited

7. Which is the smallest square?

A

C

B

D

8. Which shape belongs to this group?

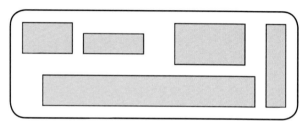

A

C

B

D

9. The objects are placed in a regular pattern. What comes next?

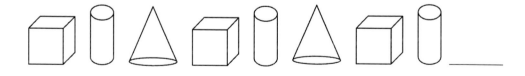

A

C

B

D

Primary Mathematics (Standards Edition) Tests 1A

10. Which two shapes form a circle?

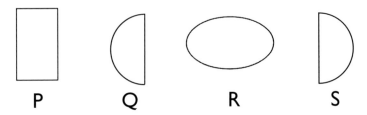

P      Q      R      S

**A**   P and Q      **C**   Q and S

**B**   R and S      **D**   P and R

# Cumulative Test A — Units 1–7

1. What is 2 less than ● ● ● ●?

   The answer is _____ .

2. # J U M P I N G

   1st

   (a) The 7th letter is _____ .

   (b) The fifth letter is _____ .

3.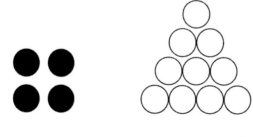

   4 + 10 = _____

4. Write the missing number.

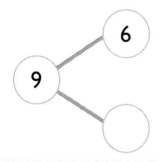

Primary Mathematics (Standards Edition) Tests 1A

5. Make addition and subtraction sentences.

3 + 4 = _____

_____ − 5 = 2

6. Count backwards by 2's.
   Write the missing numbers.

15 ( ) 11 9 ( )

7. Color the box with the greatest number.

17    11    20    15    13

8. Color the box with the smallest number.

12    19    17    13    14

9. Janice bought 14 tomatoes.
   She ate 5 of them.

   14 − 5 = _____

   She had _____ tomatoes left.

10. Subtract 2 from 20.

    The answer is _____.

11. Subtract 3 from 17.

    The answer is _____.

12. 9 + 3 = _____

13. 17 − 9 = _____

14. Color the object that can be stacked.

15. Look at the shape below.

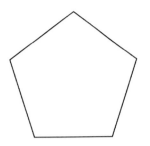

It has _____ sides.

16. The shapes are placed in a regular pattern.
    Color the shape that comes next.

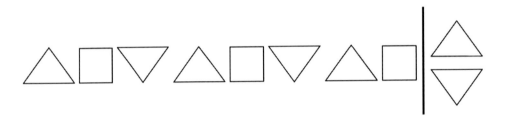

17. Match the objects to their correct shapes.

•          •          •          •


•          •          •          •

            rectangle

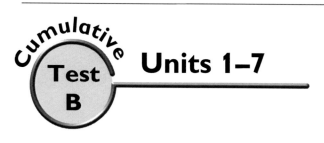

# Cumulative Test B — Units 1–7

Circle the correct option, **A**, **B**, **C** or **D**.

1. There are 7 bumblebees.
   5 more join them.
   There are _____ bumblebees now.

   **A**  10          **C**  12
   **B**  11          **D**  13

2. 11 is _____ more than 7.

   **A**  2           **C**  5
   **B**  4           **D**  7

3. 5 less than 15 is _____.

   **A**  8           **C**  10
   **B**  9           **D**  11

4. Subtract 3 from 20.
   The answer is _____.

   **A**  16          **C**  18
   **B**  17          **D**  19

Primary Mathematics (Standards Edition) Tests 1A

5. How many more marbles do we need to have 20 marbles in the box?

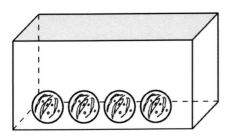

**A** 13       **C** 16

**B** 15       **D** 19

6. How many triangles are there?

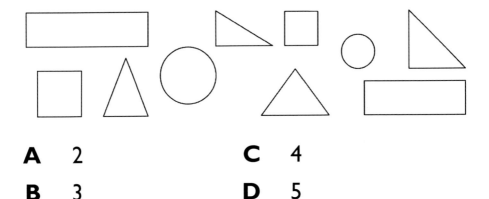

**A** 2       **C** 4

**B** 3       **D** 5

7. Which object can we stack?

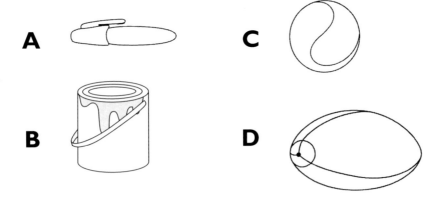

**A**

**B**

**C**

**D**

Primary Mathematics (Standards Edition) Tests 1A

© 2008 Marshall Cavendish International (Singapore) Private Limited

8. A  and a _____ have the same number of sides and corners.

A

C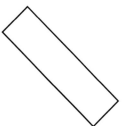

B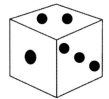

D

9. Which one of these objects does **not** have a flat surface?

A

C

B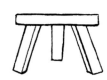

D

10. These objects are placed in a regular pattern.
    Which object comes next?

**A**         **C** ABC

**B**        **D**

**10**

**Test A**    **Unit 8:** Length

**Chapter 1:** Comparing Length

1. Color the shorter object.

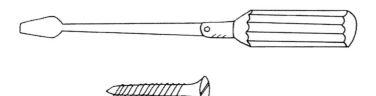

2. Color the longer brush.

3. Color the taller boy.      4. Color the shorter dog.

5. Color the longest ribbon.

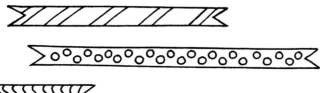

6. Color the tallest bottle.

7. Color the shortest snake.

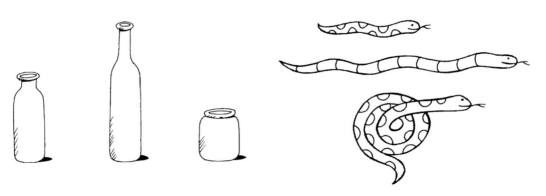

8. Arrange the animals in order.
   Begin with the shortest.

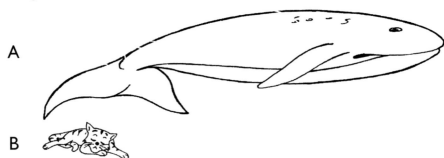

A

B

C

D

(a) _____ , _____ , _____ , _____
    shortest

(b) Animal _____ is longer than Animal C.

Primary Mathematics (Standards Edition) Tests 1A

© 2008 Marshall Cavendish International (Singapore) Private Limited

## Test B  Unit 8: Length
### Chapter 1: Comparing Length

Circle the correct option, **A**, **B**, **C** or **D**.

1.  The toothbrush is as long as the _____.

                                toothbrush

                                  pencil

                                  ruler

                                  straw

                                  paintbrush

   **A**    pencil          **C**    ruler

   **B**    straw          **D**    paintbrush

2.  Which is the tallest candle?

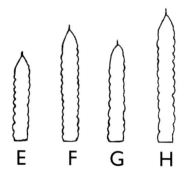

  E    F    G    H

   **A**    Candle E       **C**    Candle G

   **B**    Candle F       **D**    Candle H

Primary Mathematics (Standards Edition) Tests 1A

3. Which is the shortest arrow?

A Arrow A

B Arrow B

C Arrow C

D Arrow D

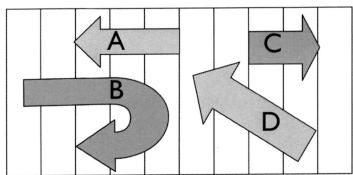

4. The pen is shorter than the _____.

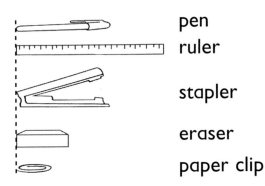

pen

ruler

stapler

eraser

paper clip

A stapler　　C eraser

B paper clip　　D ruler

5. Bree is taller than _____.

Awan　Ling　Max　Bree　Jose

A Awan　　C Ling

B Jose　　D Max

Test
A

**Unit 8:** Length

**Chapter 2:** Measuring Length

1.  Which object is taller,
    the glass or the bottle?

    The _____ .

2.  Fill in the blanks.

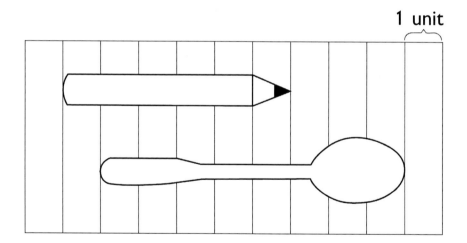

(a)  The pencil is _____ units long.

(b)  The spoon is _____ units long.

Primary Mathematics (Standards Edition) Tests 1A

3.  Each  stands for 1 unit.

 caterpillar

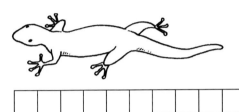 worm

lizard

(a) The caterpillar is about _____ units long.

(b) The lizard is about _____ units long.

(c) The longest animal is the _____.

4.

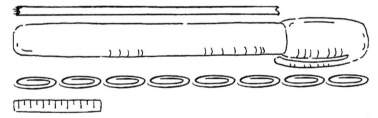

(a) The ribbon is about _____  long.

(b) The ribbon is about _____ 〔▭〕 long.

(c) The pen is about _____  long.

(d) The pen is about _____ 〔▭〕 long.

Primary Mathematics (Standards Edition) Tests 1A

© 2008 Marshall Cavendish International (Singapore) Private Limited

**Test B**  **Unit 8:** Length

**Chapter 2:** Measuring Length

Circle the correct option, **A**, **B**, **C** or **D**.

1.

✓ Mark is as tall as _____ boxes.

**A**  1          **C**  3

**B**  2          **(D)**  4

2. ✓

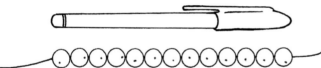

The pen is about _____ ○ long.

**A**  7          **C**  10

**B**  8          **(D)**  13

3. ✓

The straw is about _____ ⬭ long.

**A**  3          **C**  7

**B**  5          **(D)**  9

4.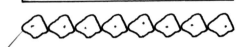

The ruler is about _____ ⬠ long.

**A** 5          **C** 8

**B** 7          **D** 9

5.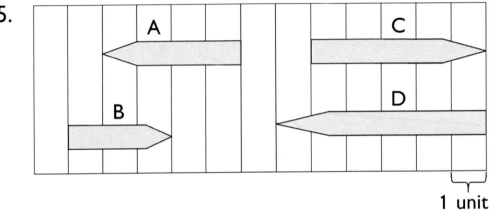

1 unit

Which is the shortest crayon?

**A** Crayon A          **C** Crayon C

**B** Crayon B          **D** Crayon D

100%

Primary Mathematics (Standards Edition) Tests 1A

© 2008 Marshall Cavendish International (Singapore) Private Limited

**Test A**

# Unit 9: Weight

## Chapter 1: Comparing Weight

1.  Circle the heavier object.

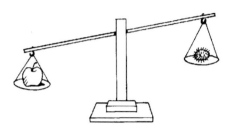

2.  Circle the lighter object.

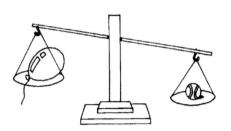

3.  Fill in the blanks.

Box _____ is lighter than Box _____.

4.  Color the heavier object.

A bucket of water          A cup of water

Use the words to answer questions 5 to 8.

| as heavy as | lighter than | heavier than |

5.  A balloon is _____ a television set.

6.  A watermelon is _____ an orange.

7.  The feather is _____ the bird.

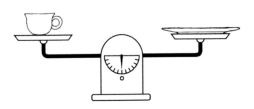

8.  The cup is _____ the plate.

9.

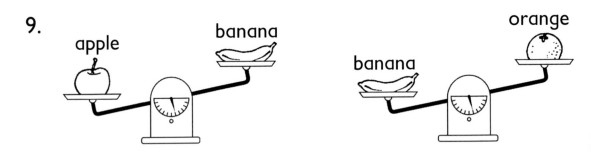

(a) The _____ is the heaviest.

(b) The _____ is the lightest.

Primary Mathematics (Standards Edition) Tests 1A

© 2008 Marshall Cavendish International (Singapore) Private Limited

**Test B**

## Unit 9: Weight

### Chapter 1: Comparing Weight

Circle the correct option, **A**, **B**, **C** or **D**.

1.

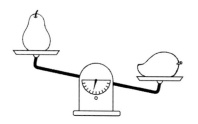

The mango is _____ the pear.

| | | | |
|---|---|---|---|
| **A** | heavier than | **C** | heaviest |
| **B** | lighter than | **D** | lightest |

2.

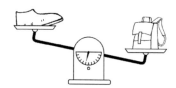

The shoe is _____ the bag.

| | | | |
|---|---|---|---|
| **A** | as heavy as | **C** | lighter than |
| **B** | heavier than | **D** | lightest |

3.

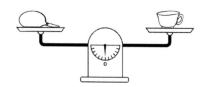

The table tennis bat is _____ the cup.

| | | | |
|---|---|---|---|
| **A** | as heavy as | **C** | heavier than |
| **B** | lighter than | **D** | heaviest |

Look at the pictures.
Answer questions 4 and 5.

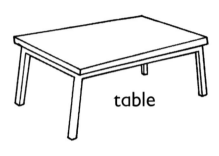 table

 stool

 basketball

 leaf

4. Which object is the lightest?

   **A**   table         **C**   basketball

   **B**   stool          **D**   leaf

5. Which object is the heaviest?

   **A**   table         **C**   basketball

   **B**   stool          **D**   leaf

# Unit 9: Weight

## Chapter 2: Measuring Weight

1. Each  stands for 1 unit.

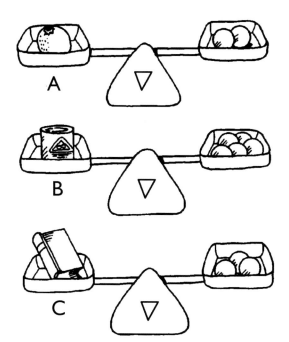

(a) Object A weighs about _____ units.

(b) Object B weighs about _____ units.

(c) Object C weighs about _____ units.

(d) Object _____ is lighter than Object C.

(e) Object _____ is heavier than Object C.

2. Each 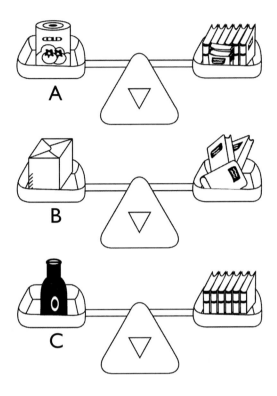 stands for 1 unit.

(a) Object _____ weighs about 6 units.

(b) Object _____ weighs about 8 units.

(c) Object C weighs more than Object _____.

(d) Object _____ is the heaviest.

(e) Object _____ is the lightest.

**Test B** — **Unit 9:** Weight

**Chapter 2:** Measuring Weight

Circle the correct option, **A**, **B**, **C** or **D**.

1. The book weighs about \_\_\_\_\_O.

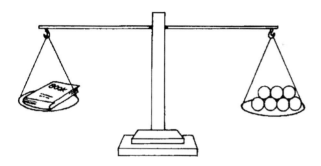

| | | | |
|---|---|---|---|
| **A** | 6 | **C** | 8 |
| **B** | 7 | **D** | 9 |

2. The bottle weighs about \_\_\_\_\_ .

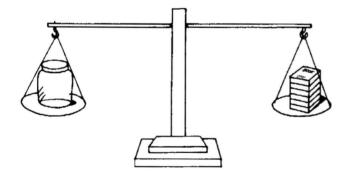

| | | | |
|---|---|---|---|
| **A** | 4 | **C** | 6 |
| **B** | 5 | **D** | 7 |

3. The mango weighs about _____ 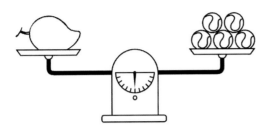.

A   2                   C   4
B   3                   D   5

4. Which is the lightest tin?

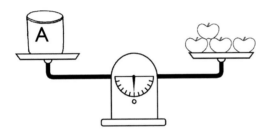

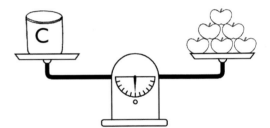

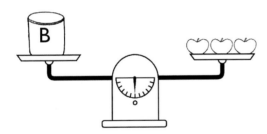

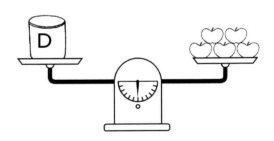

A   Tin A              C   Tin C
B   Tin B              D   Tin D

Primary Mathematics (Standards Edition) Tests 1A

**5.**

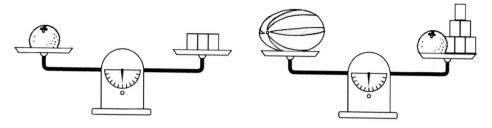

## Which is the heaviest?

**A**

**C**

**B**

**D**

Primary Mathematics (Standards Edition) Tests 1A

Blank

**Test A**

# Unit 10: Capacity

## Chapter 1: Comparing Capacity

1.

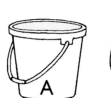  

   (a)  Bucket _____ holds the most water.

   (b)  Bucket _____ holds the least water.

   (c)  Bucket _____ holds more water than Bucket B.

2.

   Check ☑ to show which container holds more.

   ☐                ☐

3.

(a) Container _____ holds the least water.

(b) Container _____ holds the most water.

(c) Container _____ holds less water than
Container A.

4.

jugs

tub

flasks

tub

(a) It takes _____ jugs to fill the tub.

(b) It takes _____ flasks to fill the tub.

(c) Color the container that holds less.

Blank

**Test B**

# Unit 10: Capacity

## Chapter 1: Comparing Capacity

Circle the correct option, **A**, **B**, **C** or **D**.

1. _____ has the most juice.

   **A**   Gracie

   **B**   Sofia

   **C**   Charlie

   **D**   Jim

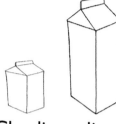

Gracie     Sofia     Charlie     Jim

Look at the picture.

Answer questions 2 and 3.

E      F      G      H

2. Container _____ can hold the least water.

   **A**   E      **B**   F      **C**   G      **D**   H

3. Container _____ can hold more than Container H.

   **A**   E      **B**   F      **C**   G      **D**   H

Look at the picture.
Answer questions 4 and 5.

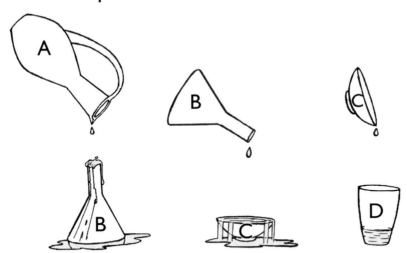

4. Which container holds the most water?

   **A**   Container A      **C**   Container C

   **B**   Container B      **D**   Container D

5. Which container holds the least water?

   **A**   Container A      **C**   Container C

   **B**   Container B      **D**   Container D

Primary Mathematics (Standards Edition) Tests 1A

**Test A**  **Unit 10:** Capacity

**Chapter 2:** Measuring Capacity

1.      beakers

(a)  It takes _____ beakers to fill Container A.

(b)  It takes _____ beakers to fill Container C.

(c)  It takes _____ beakers to fill Container D.

(d)  Container _____ can hold the most water.

(e)  Container _____ can hold the least water.

(f)  Container D can hold more water than

Container _____.

2. 

cups

jug

cups

bowl

jugs

bucket

(a) The jug can hold _____ cups of water.

(b) The bowl can hold _____ cups of water.

(c) Two jugs can hold _____ cups of water.

(d) The bucket can hold _____ cups of water.

**Test B**

**Unit 10:** Capacity

**Chapter 2:** Measuring Capacity

Circle the correct option, **A**, **B**, **C** or **D**.

Look at the picture.
Answer questions 1 and 2.

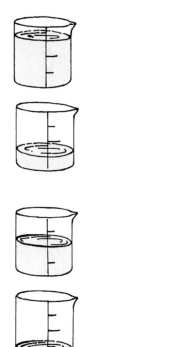

P

Q

R

S

1. Which container can hold the least water?

   **A**  Container P      **C**  Container R

   **B**  Container Q      **D**  Container S

2. _____ can hold the most water.

   **A**  Container P      **C**  Container R

   **B**  Container Q      **D**  Container S

Look at the picture.
Answer questions 3 to 5.

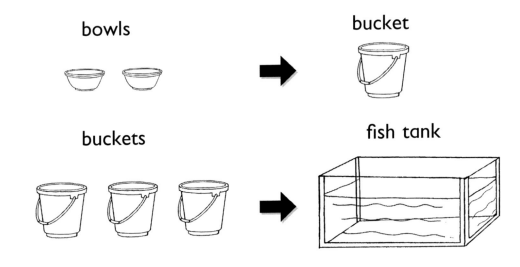

bowls

bucket

buckets

fish tank

3.  It takes _____ bowl(s) of water to fill a bucket.

    **A**  1               **C**  3

    **B**  2               **D**  4

4.  It takes _____ bucket(s) of water to fill the fish tank.

    **A**  1               **C**  3

    **B**  2               **D**  4

5.  Which container holds the most water?

    **A**  1 bowl          **C**  1 bucket

    **B**  2 bowls         **D**  1 fish tank

Primary Mathematics (Standards Edition) Tests 1A

© 2008 Marshall Cavendish International (Singapore) Private Limited

**Cumulative Test A** **Units 1–10**

1. Write **+** or **–** in each ◯.

   12 ◯ 6 = 6

   12 ◯ 3 = 15

   18 ◯ 9 = 9

   18 ◯ 2 = 20

2. Complete the addition sentences.

   6 + 8 = _____

   9 + 8 = _____

3. Color the 6th slice of watermelon from the right.

4. Count backwards.
   Write the missing numbers.

   _____, 18, 16, _____, 12, _____, 8

5. 15 − 9 = _____

6. Look at the picture carefully and fill in the blank.

   There are _____ triangles in the picture.

7. Color the shape that has 3 corners.

Primary Mathematics (Standards Edition) Tests 1A

8. Fill in the blanks.

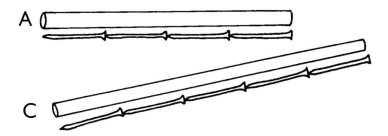

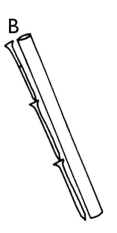

(a) Rod A is about _____ 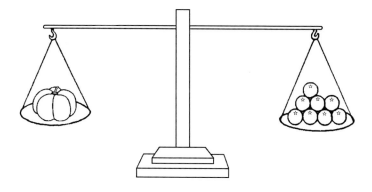 long.

(b) Rod B is about _____ long.

(c) Rod C is about _____ long.

(d) Rod A is longer than Rod _____.

(e) Rod _____ is the shortest.

9.

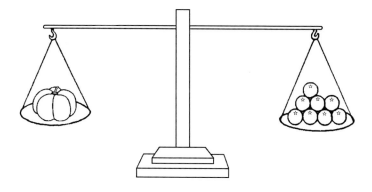

The pumpkin weighs about _____ ⊙.

Primary Mathematics (Standards Edition) Tests 1A

10. watermelon    lemon        lime

lemon

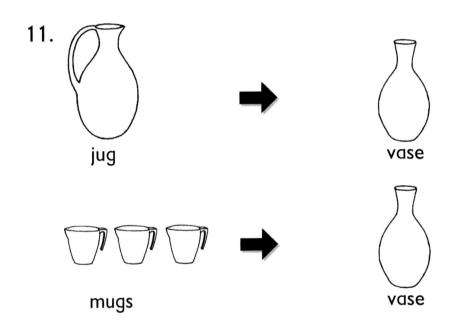

(a) The _____ is the lightest.

(b) The _____ is the heaviest.

(c) The lemon is heavier than the _____.

11.

jug

vase

mugs

vase

(a) It takes _____ jug(s) to fill the vase.

(b) It takes _____ mugs to fill the vase.

(c) A jug of water holds as much water

as _____ mugs.

Primary Mathematics (Standards Edition) Tests 1A    © 2008 Marshall Cavendish International (Singapore) Private Limited

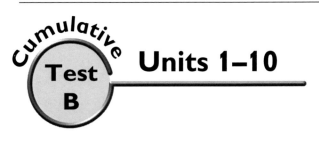

## Cumulative Test B — Units 1–10

Circle the correct option, **A**, **B**, **C** or **D**.

1. What is the missing number?

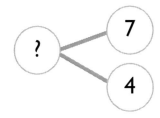

| | |
|---|---|
| **A** 10 | **C** 12 |
| **B** 11 | **D** 13 |

2. There are 6 spacecrafts.
6 more join them.

There are _____ spacecrafts now.

| | |
|---|---|
| **A** 12 | **C** 16 |
| **B** 13 | **D** 17 |

3. 16 is made up of 1 ten and _____ ones.

| | |
|---|---|
| **A** 3 | **C** 6 |
| **B** 5 | **D** 7 |

4. 14 − 5 = _____

| | |
|---|---|
| **A** 3 | **C** 7 |
| **B** 5 | **D** 9 |

Primary Mathematics (Standards Edition) Tests 1A

5. Rita had 19 erasers.
   She gave away 6 erasers.
   She has _____ erasers left.

   A   5                    C   10

   B   8                    D   13

6. 19 is _____ more than 7.

   A   11                   C   14

   B   12                   D   15

7. The numbers form a regular pattern.
   What is the missing number?

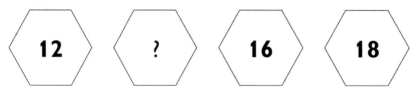

   A   13                   C   15

   B   14                   D   17

8. How many rectangles are there?

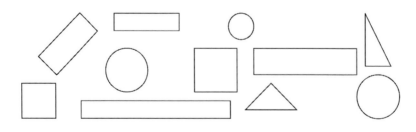

   A   1                    C   3

   B   2                    D   4

Primary Mathematics (Standards Edition) Tests 1A        © 2008 Marshall Cavendish International (Singapore) Private Limited

9. Which one of these objects has flat surfaces **only**?

A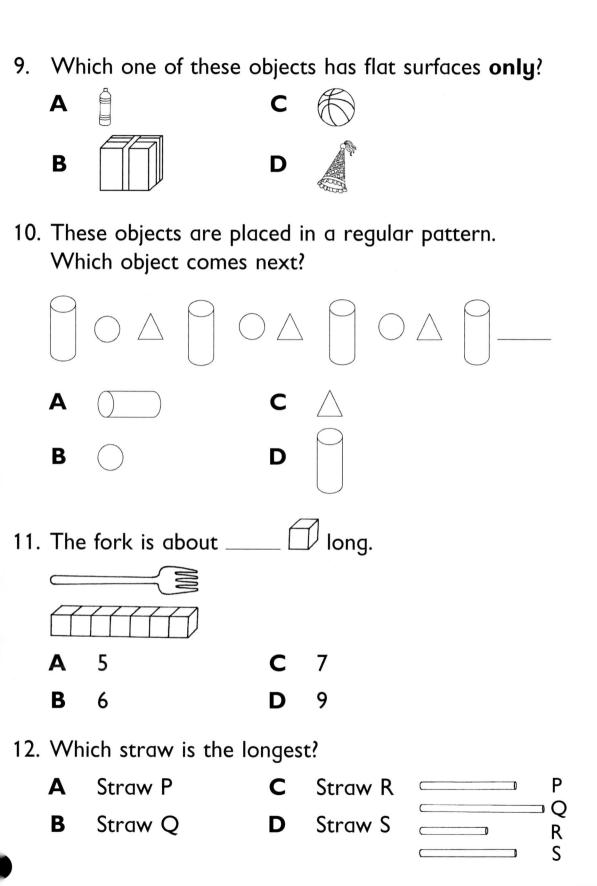

C

B

D

10. These objects are placed in a regular pattern.
Which object comes next?

A

C

B

D

11. The fork is about _____ long.

A 5

C 7

B 6

D 9

12. Which straw is the longest?

A Straw P

C Straw R

B Straw Q

D Straw S

P
Q
R
S

Primary Mathematics (Standards Edition) Tests 1A

13. Who is the tallest?

Adan   Gordon   Ling   Alisha

**A**   Adan          **C**   Ling

**B**   Gordon        **D**   Alisha

14. Which object is the heaviest?

**A**   pencil        **C**   bicycle

**B**   shoe          **D**   T-shirt

Look at the pictures.
Answer questions 15 and 16.

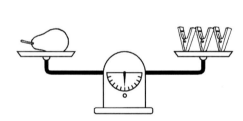   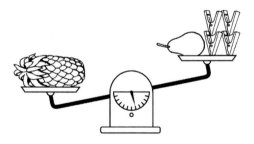

15. The weight of the pear is about _____ clothespins.

**A**   2             **C**   6

**B**   3             **D**   7

16. The _____ is/are the heaviest.

**A**   pear          **C**   3 clothespins

**B**   pineapple     **D**   4 clothespins

Primary Mathematics (Standards Edition) Tests 1A          © 2008 Marshall Cavendish International (Singapore) Private Limited

Look at the pictures.
Answer questions 17 and 18.

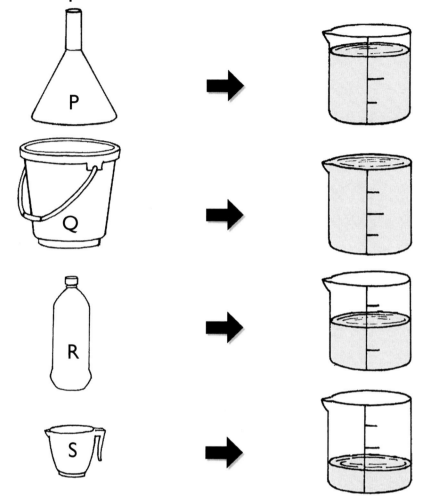

17. Which container holds the most water?

   **A**   Container P     **C**   Container R

   **B**   Container Q     **D**   Container S

18. Which container holds the least water?

   **A**   Container P     **C**   Container R

   **B**   Container Q     **D**   Container S

Primary Mathematics (Standards Edition) Tests 1A

Look at the pictures.
Answer questions 19 and 20.

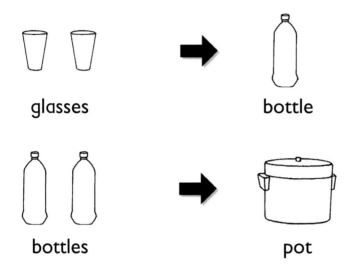

glasses → bottle

bottles → pot

19. It takes _____ bottles to fill the pot.

   **A**  1          **C**  3

   **B**  2          **D**  4

20. It takes _____ glasses to fill the pot.

   **A**  1          **C**  3

   **B**  2          **D**  4

Primary Mathematics (Standards Edition) Tests 1A

# Answers

Each question is worth 1 point unless otherwise shown in brackets [ ].

## Unit 1: Numbers 0 to 10

### Chapter 1 • Test A

1. 6; 9  [2]
2. Color 8 stars.
3. Color '4'.
4. 7
5. (a) 10  [1]
   (b) 7  [1]
   (c) Robots  [1]
6. 9; 5  [2]

### Chapter 1 • Test B

1. A   2. C   3. C   4. A   5. C
6. A   7. A   8. B   9. C   10. D

## Unit 2: Number Bonds

### Chapter 1 • Test A

1. 3
2. Draw 3 apples.
3. 6
4. Color '1' and '3'.
5.

 [4]

6. 9
7. 7

### Chapter 1 • Test B

1. C   2. B   3. C   4. A   5. A
6. C   7. B   8. A   9. D   10. A

## Units 1–2 • Cumulative Test A

1. Check 'Five'.
2. Four
3. Color 6 cups.
4. Check the set of butterflies.
5. Check the set of ducks.
6. (a) Draw a line to separate into 4 and 3.  [1]
   (b) Draw a line to separate into 1 and 2.  [1]
7. Draw 2 apples.
8. 3
9. 8, 6, 5  [3]
10. Color '3 and 1'.
11. Color '4' and '3.'
12. Color '7' and '2'.
13. 6
14. (a) 4  [1]
    (b) 5  [1]
    (c) 2  [1]
    (d) 6  [1]

## Units 1–2 • Cumulative Test B

1. B   2. B   3. C   4. A   5. C
6. A   7. D   8. C   9. D   10. B

## Unit 3: Addition

### Chapter 1 • Test A

1. 9
2. (a) 7  [1]
   (b) 9  [1]
3. 4 + 4 = 8
   3 + 5 = 8
   * Accept all possible answers.

### Chapter 1 • Test B

1. C   2. B   3. A   4. C   5. B

### Chapter 2 • Test A

1. 8
2. Draw 3 hearts; 3
3. 3
4. Draw 2 flags; 3 and 2  [2]
5. (a) 1  [1]
   (b) 5  [1]
   (c) 2  [1]
6. 9; 9  [2]

### Chapter 2 • Test B

1. B   2. C   3. A   4. B   5. D

### Chapter 3 • Test A

1. 3
2. 9
3. 5 + 3 = 8 or 3 + 5 = 8  [2]
4. Color '7'.
5. (a) 7  [1]
   (b) 9  [1]
   (c) 7  [1]
   (d) 9  [1]
6. 9
7. (a) 9  [1]
   (b) 2  [1]
   (c) 5  [1]
   (d) 4  [1]
8. 8; 8

### Chapter 3 • Test B

1. D   2. D   3. A   4. C   5. A
6. D   7. A   8. D   9. C   10. D

## Units 1–3 • Cumulative Test A

1. 10, 7
2. 7
3. 5; 3; 8  [3]
4. Draw 6 crescent moons; 6
5. 2 + 3 = 5  [2]

6. 5; 9   [2]
7. 10
8. 8
9. 6
10. 9
11. 10
12. (a) 3   [1]
    (b) 6   [1]
    (c) 5   [1]
13. 3, 0 or 0, 3   [1]
    2, 1 or 1, 2   [1]

### Units 1–3 • Cumulative Test B

1. A   2. C   3. D   4. D   5. C
6. A   7. D   8. D   9. B   10. B

### Unit 4: Subtraction

#### Chapter 1 • Test A

1. 5
2. 5
3. 3
4. $7 - \underline{2} = \underline{5}$; 5   [2]
5. $\underline{6} - 4 = \underline{2}$; 2   [2]
6. $\underline{5} - \underline{3} = \underline{2}$; 2   [3]

#### Chapter 1 • Test B

1. C   2. B   3. C   4. C   5. C

#### Chapter 2 • Test A

1. 3
2. $5 \underline{-} 2 = \underline{3}$; 3   [2]
3. 5
4. 3
5. (a) 0   [1]
   (b) 2   [1]
   (c) 4   [1]
   (d) 4   [1]
   (e) 6   [1]

#### Chapter 2 • Test B

1. B   2. A   3. B   4. A   5. D

### Units 1–4 • Cumulative Test A

1. 5, 7
2. 3
3. 5
4. Draw 1 triangle; 1
5. 6
6. 7
7. (a) 10 [1]
   (b) 6 [1]
   (c) 3 [1]
   (d) 3 [1]

8. Color '7' and '2'.
9. $\underline{4} + 5 = 9$   [1]
   $1 + \underline{9} = 10$   [1]
10. $\underline{10} - 9 = 1$   [1]
    $\underline{3} - 2 = 1$ or $\underline{2} - \underline{1} = 1$   [1]

### Units 1–4 • CumulativeTest B

1. B   2. B   3. B   4. D   5. A
6. C   7. A   8. A   9. C   10. C

### Unit 5: Position

#### Chapter 1 • Test A

1. (a) D   [1]
   (b) A   [1]
   (c) near   [1]
   (d) far from   [1]
2. (a) up   [1]
   (b) down   [1]
3. (a) under   [1]
   (b) left   [1]
   (c) right   [1]
   (d) next to   [1]

#### Chapter 1 • Test B

1. B   2. D   3. A   4. B   5 D

#### Chapter 2 • Test A

1. Color the 6th house.
2. Color the 3rd tree.
3. Draw a fish in the 3rd bowl.
4. Color the fifth bucket.
5. Color the 1st flag.
6. Circle the eighth bird.
7. (a)

[2]
   (b) first, second, third, fourth   [2]

#### Chapter 2 • Test B

1. C   2. B   3. C   4. A   5. A

### Units 1–5 • Cumulative Test A

1. 7
2. 8
3. 2
4. 9, 4
5. 6

6. $3 + \underline{2} = \underline{5}$ [1]
   $\underline{5} - 3 = \underline{2}$ [1]
7. (a) 9 [1]
   (b) 9 [1]
   (c) 4 [1]
   (d) 4 [1]
8. (a) left [1]
   (b) under [1]
   (c) right [1]
   (d) above [1]
9. Color the 5th triangle.
10. Color the 4th ball.
11. (a) 3rd [1]
    (b) ninth [1]
    (c) sixth [1]

## Units 1–5 • Cumulative Test B

1. C   2. C   3. D   4. A   5. D
6. C   7. D   8. B   9. C   10. A
11. D  12. C  13. C  14. C  15. A

## Unit 6: Numbers to 20

### Chapter 1 • Test A

1. (a) Check '12'. [1]
   (b) Check 'eighteen'. [1]
2. Color 10 triangles; 3
3. 19, 17
4. Color '18'.
5. 9, 11, 15, 16 [2]
6. 18
7. 10
8. 10

### Chapter 1 • Test B

1. D   2. C   3. B   4. B   5. A
6. D   7. B   8. C   9. C   10. B

### Chapter 2 • Test A

1. 2,1 or 1,2 [1]
   11 [1]
2. (a) 18 [1]
   (b) 10 [1]
3. (a) + [1]
   (b) - [1]
   (c) + [1]
   (d) - [1]
4. 13
5. 8
6. 6,10 or 10,6 [1]
   9 [1]
7. 9
8. 15; 15
9. 9; 9

### Chapter 2 • Test B

1. C   2. D   3. C   4. D   5. A
6. D   7. A   8. B   9. C   10. B

## Units 1–6 • Cumulative Test A

1. 3
2. Color '4 and 3'.
3. 7
4. $5 + \underline{3} = 8$
   $3 + \underline{5} = 8$
5. Color the 3rd ball.
6. (a) 12, 16 [1]
   (b) 20, 17 [1]
7. 4
8. 18
9. (a) 14 [1]
   (b) 19 [1]
   (c) 12 [1]
   (d) 7 [1]
10. 20
11. 5

## Units 1–6 • Cumulative Test B

1. C   2. C   3. D   4. A   5. B
6. C   7. A   8. D   9. C   10. A

## Unit 7: Shapes

### Chapter 1 • Test A

1. Color the rectangle.
   Color the circle.
2. Color the bigger circle.
3. Check the sphere.
4.
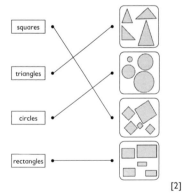
5. Check the book and tissue box.
6.

[2]
7. Color the hexagon.
8. Color the marble.
9. Color the 2 triangles.

Primary Mathematics (Standards Edition) Tests 1A

## Chapter 1 • Test B

1.  C    2.  B    3.  A    4.  D    5.  C
6.  A    7.  A    8.  D    9.  B    10. C

### Units 1–7 • Cumulative Test A

1.  2
2.  (a) G    [1]
    (b) I    [1]
3.  14
4.  3
5.  3 + 4 = 7    [1]
    7 − 5 = 2    [1]
6.  13, 7    [1]
7.  Color '20'.
8.  Color '12'.
9.  9, 9
10. 18
11. 14
12. 12
13. 8
14. Color the plate.
15. 5
16. Color
17.

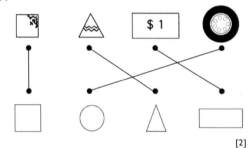

[2]

### Units 1–7 • Cumulative Test B

1.  C    2.  B    3.  C    4.  B    5.  C
6.  C    7.  B    8.  C    9.  B    10. A

### Unit 8: Length

#### Chapter 1 • Test A

1.  Color the nail.
2.  Color the longer brush.
3.  Color the taller boy.
4.  Color the shorter dog.
5.  Color the longest ribbon.
6.  Color the tallest bottle.
7.  Color the shortest snake.
8.  (a) D, B, C, A    [2]
    (b) A    [1]

## Chapter 1 • Test B

1.  B    2.  D    3.  C    4.  D    5.  B

### Chapter 2 • Test A

1.  bottle
2.  (a) 6    [1]
    (b) 8    [1]
3.  (a) 7    [1]
    (b) 9    [1]
    (c) worm    [1]
4.  (a) 6    [1]
    (b) 3    [1]
    (c) 8    [1]
    (d) 4    [1]

### Chapter 2 • Test B

1.  D    2.  D    3.  D    4.  C    5.  B

### Unit 9: Weight

#### Chapter 1 • Test A

1.  Circle the apple.
2.  Circle the balloon.
3.  B, A
4.  Color the bucket.
5.  lighter than
6.  heavier than
7.  lighter than
8.  as heavy as
9.  (a) apple    [1]
    (b) orange    [1]

#### Chapter 1 • Test B

1.  A    2.  C    3.  A    4.  D    5.  A

#### Chapter 2 • Test A

1.  (a) 2    [1]
    (b) 5    [1]
    (c) 3    [1]
    (d) A    [1]
    (e) B    [1]
2.  (a) C    [1]
    (b) A    [1]
    (c) B    [1]
    (d) A    [1]
    (e) B    [1]

#### Chapter 2 • Test B

1.  B    2.  C    3.  D    4.  B    5.  C

### Unit 10: Capacity

#### Chapter 1 • Test A

1.  (a) C    [1]
    (b) A    [1]
    (c) C    [1]
2.  Check the flask on the left.

3. (a) B  [1]
   (b) C  [1]
   (c) B  [1]
4. (a) 16  [1]
   (b) 10  [1]
   (c) Color the jug on the left.  [1]

## Chapter 1 • Test B

1.  D    2.  B    3.  C    4.  A    5.  C

## Chapter 2 • Test A

1. (a)  4  [1]
   (b)  8  [1]
   (c)  3  [1]
   (d)  C  [1]
   (e)  B  [1]
   (f)  B  [1]
2. (a)  2  [1]
   (b)  4  [1]
   (c)  4  [1]
   (d)  6  [1]

## Chapter 2 • Test B

1.  D    2.  A    3.  B    4.  C    5.  D

## Units 1–10 • Cumulative Test A

1.  -, +, -, +   [4]
2.  14, 17   [2]
3.  Color the 1st slice of watermelon.
4.  20, 14, 10  [3]
5.  6
6.  16
7.  Color the triangle.
8. (a) 4  [1]
   (b) 3  [1]
   (c) 5  [1]
   (d) B  [1]
   (e) B  [1]
9.  8
10. (a) lime         [1]
    (b) watermelon   [1]
    (c) lime         [1]
11. (a) 1  [1]
    (b) 3  [1]
    (c) 3  [1]

## Units 1–10 • Cumulative Test B

1.  B    2.  A    3.  C    4.  D    5.  D
6.  B    7.  B    8.  D    9.  B   10.  B
11. C   12.  B   13.  C   14.  C   15.  B
16. B   17.  B   18.  D   19.  B   20.  D

Blank